VEGETARIAN FOODSCAPE

VEGETARIAN FOODSCAPE

Celia Brooks Brown

designed by Julia Dunlop

Pen & Ink
10 Foundry Street
Brighton
East Sussex   BN1 4AT
Tel. (01273) 600229
email: juliad@pen-and-ink.demon.co.uk

Front cover illustration by Jessica Brown
Still Life with Aubergine (1998)
Oil on cedar panel
Courtesy of Elizabeth O'Neil

Published by Pen & Ink
© Celia Brooks Brown 1998

Special thanks to Rosie Kindersley, Julia Brock and Livvy Mason

ISBN 0 9534022 0 7

Printed and bound by
MPG Books Ltd.
Victoria Square
Bodmin
Cornwall   PL3 1EG

for Christiane Kubrick

CONTENTS

STUFFED FAVOURITES...

MAJOR DISHES...

VARIATIONS ON CLASSICS...

ACCOMPANIMENTS...

SWEETS...

FOREWORD

I call myself a natural-born vegetarian because I have never liked the taste of meat or fish. Having grown up in the USA, I thrived on junk food, and cooking was always an anathema to me. I didn't have any gastronomic inspiration early on: for my mother, cooking was a chore, not a pleasure, and my idea of a culinary delight at my grandmother's house was white Rainbo bread smothered in Miracle Whip, a fake mayonnaise, as I wasn't allowed this sort of food at home.

Things began to change when I moved to England at the age of nineteen pursuing a career as a theatre director. Before long I stumbled upon a part-time job posing as a life model for painter Christiane Kubrick. She would send me to the well-stocked kitchen at lunchtime to throw a couple of potatoes in the AGA, and I stood petrified with ignorance. Soon I forced myself to overcome my fear. I discovered the fun of creating beautiful plated dishes using the shapes and colours of vegetables and fruits as a palette. Mrs. Kubrick and various 'guinea pigs' were extremely patient with me while I developed basic culinary skills. Eventually I took on the challenge of cooking for large groups.

Before long I was so besotted with cooking that it entirely replaced the theatre as the main creative endeavour in my life. They are similar art forms: starting with a good script or menu, one must bring together all the elements and create a performance out of them within a time frame. Inevitably, it ends up rather frantic and pressurised toward the end, but this fervour adds to the flavour of the final result. The curtain goes up, and a hopefully appreciative audience gobble up the goodies. Once it's over, it's just a memory, but it remains in the heart.

Cooking, however, is much more than an art form. Whether for family, friends or clients, it's a labour of love which makes one feel human in this distracting world of ours. In the kitchen, we entertain all the elements. Fire, water in all its states, and air: hot or cold, it changes our food. The earth bears our ingredients and the metals, woods and clays of our tools. All five senses go to work as well; the smells and tastes, of course, but also what we see, hear and touch. Ultimately we satiate our foremost need for survival, to eat!

The first day I walked into Books for Cooks divides my life into Then and Now. I realised I had arrived in a cook's paradise, as so many people who visit and revisit Books for Cooks do. But mostly it confirmed the beginning of an odyssey. I started working as a bookseller, with my eye on cooking in the 16-seat restaurant. Within a year I was cooking here once a week, as well as cooking freelance. Books for Cooks is the Oracle of the British food world, and from here answers, opinions, passions, history and divine fragrances and flavours all radiate. This is my base, and now I'm channelling my good fortune into this book of my best early recipes. I hope it represents a departure from vegetarian "funda*lentil*ism" which still has its finger on the pulse.

NOTES

Aubergines: I'd like to clear the air concerning the debate over whether or not to salt aubergines before cooking. If the aubergines contain bitter juices, the salt will draw them out, but it appears that this tongue-tickling quality of the juice has been bred out of the modern aubergine. Salting also affects the cooking, depending on which method you're using. When salted, their flesh contracts, and will therefore absorb less oil when fried. So if you're frying them, you'll get a crisper result if you salt them first. If you're char-grilling or baking them, however, don't salt them, or they will be too dry and flimsy.

Chillies: I keep a box of latex examination gloves (available from any chemist) in the kitchen for the sole purpose of handling chillies. Capsaicin, the fiery chemical in the chilli flesh and concentrated in the seeds is a remarkable substance. It will penetrate the skin and tough fingers might not feel it; transfer it from fingers to eyes or other sensitive parts, and you'll regret it. It has the same effect on the tongue, of course, and those who find pleasure in this sensation have been known to go to extremes of worship, especially in the US where you'll find chilli shops, chilli festivals, and chilli products with names like "Spontaneous Combustion." There is evidence that capsaicin not only has anti-bacterial effects, but that the pleasurable pain it inflicts on the palate causes the brain to release endorphins, giving us a natural high.

    Habaneros are the world's hottest chilli. Their close cousin the Scotch Bonnet is widely available in Britain. They are easily recognisable: squat, orange or red and lantern-shaped. They contain the highest concentration of capsaicin, measuring 200,000 to 300,000 Scoville units, the top of the chilli Richter scale.

Olive oil: The quality of the olive oil used determines the quality of the end result: Italian fundamentalists would argue this point vehemently. But here in England, one is likely to pay extortionate prices for a fine olive oil. My rule of thumb is, so long as it's extra virgin, it's good enough for the recipes in this book (though it would be too strongly flavoured for making mayonnaise). I save money by buying 5 litre drums of Tuscan extra virgin and siphoning it off into bottles, as I do get through oceans of the stuff.

Vegetable stock: Make your own by saving offcuts from vegetables such as peelings, superfluous greens and stems (such as from celery, leeks, broccoli or cauliflower) and herb stems, as long as they're clean and fresh. Build up a collection over a few days and store in a sealed container in the fridge, then cover with water in a pan, add salt and boil them up for half an hour or so, drain and use or freeze.

Or just throw a quartered onion into a pot with some carrot, celery or any other available vegetable and a few herbs. Always save the water you've used to blanche, steam or boil vegetables and use it to make stock; if you have room in the freezer, you can always have stock to hand.

Things to avoid: onion skins, which often give the stock a bitter taste. Do save them up around Easter, though, and boil eggs with them, as they contain a remarkably strong brown pigment. Too much potato will result in a slimy stock. And as for peelings, if you absolutely would not eat the peel, don't use it in stock (avocados, hard squashes).

Finally, there is nothing wrong with the stock-cube method, though it won't taste nearly as good as home-made. Just be sure to pick a good quality one which doesn't contain any e-nasties.

Food processors: Elizabeth David may turn in her grave, but my food processor is utterly indispensable, so a few of the recipes require its use. If you don't have one, you can use logic to get round it in some cases. There's no substitute, however, for the sheer liquidising power of the counter-top blender. When it comes to soups, I highly recommend a hand-operated blender for puréeing directly in the pot.

These compact machines are cheap to acquire and easy to clean.

Pastry: Shortcrust pastry is a doddle to make in the food processor. Just be sure the butter and water are extremely cold. For one 24 cm / 9 ½ inch case, place 180 g / 6 oz. of plain flour in the processing jug with the rotary blade. For sweet pastry, add 75 g / 2 ½ oz. icing sugar. Add a pinch of salt and pulse a few times to aerate. Add 90 g / 3 oz. well-chilled or frozen cubed butter and process until the mixture resembles fine breadcrumbs. Gradually add 3 Tbsp. ice water and wait until the pastry just draws together. Over-processing will result in tough pastry. Shape into a ball, flatten, wrap in cling film and chill for about half an hour.

Roll out the pastry on a lightly floured surface. Take care that it doesn't stick to the surface and redust underneath the pastry as you go. Roll up onto the rolling pin and lay in a fluted tin with a removable base. Press into the sides of the tin and trim with a knife. Press the sides in again so they extend slightly beyond the tin's edge; this should allow for shrinkage. Place the case in the freezer until ready to bake. It must be very cold or, even better, frozen when it goes in the oven.

Preheat the oven to 180°C / 350°F. Line the case with baking parchment and fill with baking beans, pasta or rice. Bake for 10 minutes, remove the beans, and bake a further 10 minutes. It is now baked blind and ready to fill.

SOUPS

SOPA DE AGUACATE (AVOCADO) WITH CRISP QUESADILLA TOPPING

Avocados must never be cooked or they lose the buttery succulence which makes them so very delicious. So most avocado dishes one comes across throughout the world, including soups, are served cold. But once, in Mexico, I ate an incredibly delicious hot avocado soup under a thatched hut on the beach and I have been trying to recreate it ever since. The trick is to have it warmed through but not cooked, so the avocado oils slither meltingly down the throat. Essentially it is a guacamole diluted with hot stock, and topped with crunchy, cheesy nachos—very Mexican. And you don't necessarily need the thatched hut and beach to enjoy it.

For the soup:
2 large or 4 small ripe avocados
juice of 2 limes
200 ml / 7 fl. oz. crème fraîche
1 small onion, finely chopped
2 tomatoes, chopped
1 garlic clove, crushed
1 red chilli, deseeded and finely minced
1 litre / 1 ¾ pints. hot vegetable stock
salt and pepper

For the topping:
100g / 3 ½ oz. corn tortilla chips (unflavoured)
100g / 3 ½ oz. Cheddar or Monterey Jack cheese
1 bunch spring onions, chopped

Preheat the oven to its highest setting. Scoop out the avocado flesh and mash it with the lime juice. Stir in the crème fraîche, onion, tomato, garlic, and chilli, and season to taste with salt and pepper. Now warm your serving bowls slightly.

The stock should be hot but not boiling. Stir the stock into the avocado mixture. Ladle into the warmed serving bowls. Scatter a few tortilla chips on top of each bowl and sprinkle with cheese. Pop the bowls in the oven for just a few minutes, until the cheese melts. Remove from the oven, top with a few chopped spring onions and eat immediately.

SERVES 6 -8

TOMATO AND GINGER SOUP

Preparation is kept to a minimum in this light tomato soup; no skinning or fine chopping is necessary as it all gets pushed through a sieve at the end. It's buzzing with ginger and really wakes up the palate as an appetiser. Also it contains absolutely no fat.

1.25 kg / 2 ½ lbs. fresh ripe tomatoes
600 ml / 1 pint vegetable stock
30g /1 oz. piece of fresh root ginger, peeled and roughly chopped
4 garlic cloves, peeled and roughly chopped
1-2 tsp. dark muscovado sugar, depending on the sweetness of the tomatoes
pepper and ½ tsp. salt, or to taste
a handful of chopped parsley to garnish

Wash the tomatoes and place them in a lidded pot with the stock. Cover, bring to the boil, then turn down the heat to a simmer. Meanwhile, prepare the other ingredients.

After about 10 minutes, add everything else to the pot and stir. Keep it covered and simmer for half an hour.

Let the soup cool off a bit, then purée. Now for an utterly velvety consistency, it must be pushed through a sieve. Place a sieve over a large bowl. Pour the soup in bit by bit, rubbing it through with a ladle. Taste for seasoning.

Reheat the soup in the pot and serve each bowl with chopped parsley and lashings of freshly ground black pepper.

SERVES 4-6

PEAR AND PARSNIP SOUP WITH STILTON

Fruit and cheese love each other: a lightly poached pear with grilled Stilton on top is pure ambrosia. Pears are friends with parsnips too, and all three together are a triumphant triumvirate. This is a soup which, for me, defines the joy of winter food.

60 g / 2 oz. butter
2 large onions, chopped
1 Tbsp. fresh thyme leaves
3 celery sticks, chopped
1 kg / 2 lbs. parsnips, peeled and chopped
2 pears, peeled and chopped and dressed with the
    juice of 1 lemon
salt and freshly ground pepper
1.5 litres / 2 ¾ pints vegetable stock
250 g / 8 oz. Stilton, crumbled

Melt the butter in a large pot and gently soften the onion with the thyme until translucent. Add the celery, parsnips and seasoning, cover and sweat for 10 minutes, stirring occasionally. Add the pears with the lemon juice and the stock. Bring to the boil and simmer for half an hour. Cool briefly and purée. Ladle into bowls and sprinkle crumbled Stilton on top of each. Crusty bread a must.

SERVES 6 -8

SPICED CARROT AND APPLE SOUP

Here's a richly spiced, eye-opening soup which launches the taste buds into the main course, or makes a meal of itself with bread and cheese. It's a soup which multiplies well, and if you do so, wrap the star anise up in a little piece of muslin and tie with a string, or you may not be able to fish them out before puréeing. (Do the same if you only have pieces of star anise and not whole ones.) The lime at the end is optional: you may wish to sharpen it if your carrots or apples are especially sweet. The dollop of Greek yoghurt is mandatory to conduct the symphony of flavours.

30 g / 1 oz. butter
1 large onion, chopped
3 garlic cloves, chopped
1 walnut-sized piece of fresh ginger, chopped
3 whole star anise
½ whole nutmeg, grated
1 Tbsp. coriander seeds, crushed
2 tsp. salt, or to your taste
freshly ground black pepper
800 g / 1 ½ lb. carrots, peeled and sliced
1 Granny Smith or cooking apple, peeled, cored
  and chopped
1.5 litres / 2 ¾ pints vegetable stock
juice of one lime (optional)

To serve:
Greek yoghurt
chopped mint or coriander
pita bread, cut into strips and grilled

Melt the butter in a lidded pot and soften the onion, garlic and ginger with the salt and spices over a low flame. When the onions are translucent, add the carrot and apple. Cover and sweat for 15 minutes, stirring now and then.

Pour in the stock, bring to the boil, lower the heat and simmer for 20 minutes. Remove the star anise (it should have floated to the top), and purée. Taste and sharpen with the lime juice if desired. Serve each bowl with a dollop of Greek yoghurt, and a sprinkling of fresh mint or coriander leaves, and strips of grilled pita laid on top.

SERVES 4-6

HANGOVER SOUP

There is a traditional Hungarian remedy for hangovers known as "Korhelyleves" which is a soup made with sausage and sauerkraut. My version contains a bit of the hair of the dog and rich doses of protein and vitamin C, which are truly medicinal in such circumstances. It is simple enough for a zombie to prepare in a jiffy and is made up of ingredients which are likely to be hanging around anyway-so no hobbling to the shop (hence several "optional" ingredients). It needn't be strictly prepared for a hangover, of course. Quick-cooking red lentils, or any sort of lentil, paired with lemons, are a dream-team.

200 g / 7 oz. red lentils
1 onion, chopped coarsely
2 cloves of garlic
2 Tbsp. olive oil
salt and pepper
1 litre / 1 ¾ pints vegetable stock (or 2 stock cubes dissolved in the same amount of boiling water)
grated zest and juice of 2 lemons

Optional:
1 glass of white wine (still lingering on the table?)
1 tsp. dried chilli flakes or to taste
yoghurt
chopped herbs

Wash the lentils and place in a small bowl. Cover with boiling water and leave to stand while you get on with preparing your onions and garlic; this is not essential but it will speed up the cooking process. Heat the oil in a heavy-bottomed pot and fry the onion over low to moderate heat with some salt and pepper.

When the onion is translucent, add the garlic and soaked lentils. Stir for a couple of minutes, until the lentils start to turn pale. Pour in the stock with the lemon juice and zest, and the wine and chilli, if using. Simmer for 20 minutes, stirring occasionally.

Add yoghurt and chopped herbs to each bowl for a perfect soup.

SERVES 4

PUY LENTIL, COCONUT AND WILTED SPINACH SOUP

The prized Puy lentil is best for this simple recipe, first for flavour and second for holding its shape when cooked. Baby spinach leaves bathed in the delicately spiced broth have a refreshing bite to them. If you won't be serving all the soup at once, place a small handful of spinach leaves in each bowl and ladle the hot soup over them, and they will wilt just the same.

250 g / 8 oz. Puy lentils
2 litres / 3 ¾ pints vegetable stock
1 large onion, chopped
3 fat cloves of garlic, chopped
1 Tbsp. ground cumin
150 g / 5 oz. block creamed coconut, chopped and
 dissolved in 150 ml / 5 fl oz. boiling water
2 Tbsp. soy sauce
150 g / 5 oz. baby spinach leaves
salt and pepper to taste

Rinse the lentils and place in a large pot with enough cold water just to cover them. Bring to the boil and keep them boiling vigorously for 10 minutes. Add everything else except the spinach and bring back to the boil. Simmer gently for 20 minutes to half an hour, or until the lentils are cooked. Stir in the spinach and serve immediately with warm flatbread.

SERVES 8

SALADS

SUGARBEANS

Marinating transports beans into a whole new gustatory dimension. This salad takes a long time to make, but it is well worth it. It is inspired by a recipe of my late Great Aunt Nonie in Texas, who passed her version on as a family favourite for taking along to pot luck suppers and picnics. And yes, it does contain rather a lot of sugar.

For the salad:
500g / 1 lb. mixed dry beans
200g / 7 oz. French beans or runner beans, cut into bite-sized pieces
2 X 225g / 7 ½ oz. tins water chestnuts, drained
1 green pepper, cut into bite-sized pieces
1 red onion, finely sliced

For the marinade:
125 ml / 4 fl. oz. balsamic vinegar
90g / 3 oz. caster sugar
3 garlic cloves, crushed
2 tsp. salt
125 ml / 4 fl. oz. olive oil
lots of freshly ground black pepper

Soak the dry beans in plenty of cold water overnight. Boil them up in fresh water and let them roll furiously for 10 minutes, then simmer for 50 minutes, until tender, but not falling apart. (Or follow package directions.)

Meanwhile, prepare the marinade by whisking together all ingredients except the oil. Beat in the oil gradually to prevent separation.

Two minutes before the mixed beans are finished cooking, drop in the green beans to blanch them. Drain them all thoroughly.

Empty into a wide, shallow dish and pour over the marinade while they are still hot. Add the water chestnuts, green pepper and red onion. Stir it up well. When cool, cover and refrigerate for at least 24 hours, stirring now and then. The salad will keep for several days in the refrigerator.

SERVES 10

NEW POTATO AND HALLOUMI SALAD

There are two classic schools of potato salads: one dressed in vinaigrette and one dressed in mayonnaise, yoghurt, crème fraîche or a combination of these. I normally like to keep potato salads simple and let the delicious potatoes speak for themselves with a little help from the dressing and some onion. This rather more elaborate salad has become a favourite, however, and is a meal in itself, full of varied textures, flavours and colours.

For the dressing:
150 ml / 5 fl. oz. balsamic vinegar
1 clove of garlic, chopped
1 Tbsp. honey
2 tsp. coarse grain mustard
salt and pepper
100 ml / 3 ½ fl. oz. olive oil

For the salad:
500 g / 1 lb. new potatoes, washed
1 small or ½ large red onion, halved and finely sliced
2 red peppers
250 g / 8 oz. Halloumi cheese
juice of 1 lemon
a handful of chopped mint
salad leaves

First prepare the peppers. Heat the grill or oven to the highest setting. Cut the peppers in half from stem to base and remove the stem and seeds. Place cut-side-down on a baking sheet and grill or roast until blackened and blistered all over. Remove to a plastic bag, seal and leave to sweat until cool enough to handle. Peel off and discard the papery skins and slice the flesh into strips.

Cook the potatoes in boiling, salted water until tender. Meanwhile, make the dressing. Whisk everything together except the olive oil, then gradually whisk it in. Drain the potatoes and combine with the dressing, peppers and onions while still hot.

Smear a little olive oil on the bottom of a wide frying pan and heat it over a moderate flame. Cut the Halloumi into 0.5cm / ¼ inch slices. Lay in a single layer in the pan and cook until dry and brown on the bottom, then turn over and cook the other side. As soon as it's done, squeeze the lemon juice over the cheese in the pan. Break up the cheese and stir into the potatoes. Finish with chopped mint, and serve on a bed of leaves.

SERVES 4-6

CRISPY NOODLE SALAD

This scrumptious salad is full of light, crunchy textures and zesty fusion flavours. Frying the dry noodles may seem a bit daunting, but the resulting nest is a beautiful and delicious accompaniment to any Oriental dish. The humble iceberg lettuce is frowned upon by some, but its sweetness is perfect in this main-course salad. Cos lettuce and Chinese leaf work as well. All components can be prepared in advance, but should be assembled just at the last moment to prevent sogginess.

For the salad:
125g / 4 oz. fine rice noodles
oil for deep frying
60g / 2 oz. flaked almonds, toasted
60g / 2 oz. sesame seeds
3 sticks of celery, sliced
1 bunch of spring onions, sliced diagonally
1 iceberg lettuce, cut into 2 cm / 1 inch squares,
    washed and dried
250 g / 8 oz. Halloumi cheese

For the dressing:
1 walnut-sized piece of fresh root ginger, grated
4 Tbsp. caster sugar
1 Tbsp. dark soy sauce
6 Tbsp. rice vinegar
½ tsp. ground black pepper
125ml / 4 fl. oz. olive oil

In a deep, wide pot, heat a 10 cm / 4 inch deep pool of frying oil until it begins to smoke. (The oil can be strained and reused when completely cool.) Have tongs and a large dish lined with paper towels ready next to the pot. Pull the dry noodles apart slightly so they are not tightly packed and place carefully in the oil. They will almost immediately erupt into a huge crunchy mass, and within seconds, will start to turn light golden. At this point, grasp the whole mass with tongs and drain in the lined dish.

While the noodles are cooling, make the dressing. Simply whizz everything together in the blender.

Slice the Halloumi cheese as thinly as possible. Place in a single layer in a dry frying pan on a moderate flame until the underside of the cheese is dry and brown, then flip over and brown the other side. (Do this in batches or in two pans.) Meanwhile, keeping the dressing aside, assemble the rest of the salad. Toss everything together thoroughly with your hands, breaking up the noodles as you go. While the cheese is still warm, break it up and toss in. Add the dressing last, stir well and eat right away.

SERVES 4-6

SWEET AND SOUR AUBERGINE AND GOAT'S CHEESE SALAD

It's worth having one of these fabulous cast iron ridged char-grill pans just for cooking aubergines, if nothing else. These sponge-like vegetables require a minimum amount of oil for char-grilling and come out tender and dressed in bold stripes, with a hint of smoke in the flavour. (Do turn off the fire alarm, though, and prepare for a smoke-out!) Alternatively you could fry them. The sweet and sour aubergines could play a starring role in a selection of meze such as houmous and tzatziki, stuffed into a pita. They make a complete meal when paired up with creamy warm goat's cheese on a bed of leaves. A drizzle of pomegranate molasses is the finishing touch, but is not strictly necessary; if you haven't yet discovered this mysterious condiment, hunt it down in shops selling Middle Eastern groceries.

2 large or 3 medium aubergines
60-90 ml / 2-3 fl. oz. olive oil
100 ml / 3 ½ fl. oz. dry vermouth or white wine
3 Tbsp. wine vinegar
1 ½ Tbsp. sugar
salt and pepper
200 g / 7 oz. goat's cheese, sliced into four rounds
4 tsp. pomegranate molasses
young spinach leaves
a handful of fresh mint leaves, chopped

Chop the spiky green top off the aubergines. Stand them on the severed end and slice downwards, shaving off and discarding the first and last bit of skin. Make slices 1 cm / ½ inch thick. Brush each slice on both sides with olive oil.

Cook the aubergines in batches. Heat the char-grill pan until very hot. Lay the aubergines in the pan and cook each side until translucent and striped with black. You can encourage them by pressing them into the pan with a spatula. Allow to cool slightly, then cut the cooked aubergines into long strips about 2 cm / 1 inch wide.

Heat the remaining oil in a large frying pan over moderate heat. (If you have used up all the oil, add a couple of tablespoons to the pan.) When hot, add the aubergines and spread them out evenly in the pan. Add the vermouth or wine all at once—stand back as it may splutter at first. Season well with salt and pepper and cook, stirring gently, until the wine has almost completely evaporated. Add the vinegar and sugar to the pan and stir. Cook for a couple more minutes, while the juices thicken and caramelise, then remove the pan from the heat. Transfer the aubergines to a bowl and let them cool down a bit.

Heat your grill or oven to high. Place the goat's cheese rounds on a lightly oiled baking sheet and grill or bake until just starting to soften. Meanwhile, make a bed of young spinach leaves on each plate and pile the sweet and sour aubergines on top. Finish with a warm goat's cheese round on the summit. Drizzle pomegranate molasses over the cheese and sprinkle with chopped mint.

SERVES 4

MAGIC BALSAMIC VINAIGRETTE

Everyone has their own personal favourite salad dressing, and this is mine. It has a magic ingredient, a condiment which deserves to be as much a household name as Lea & Perrins or Tabasco: Maggi Liquid Seasoning. It comes in a small brown bottle with a long neck and a yellow label and top. If you cannot find it, substitute ½tsp. sugar and ½tsp. soy sauce.

1 clove of garlic
½ tsp. coarse sea salt
60 ml / 2 fl oz. balsamic vinegar
1 tsp. Maggi Liquid Seasoning
freshly ground black pepper
100 ml / 3 ½ fl. oz. olive oil

Mash up the garlic with the salt in a mortar and pestle until smooth. Pour the vinegar into the mortar and stir: this will ensure you get every last bit of garlic essence out of the vessel. Transfer to a bowl or jug, and add the Maggi and pepper. Whisk in the oil in a slow and steady stream to emulsify.

A salad should always be dressed at the last minute, as its beauty fades fast!

WARM SALAD OF
WILD MUSHROOMS AND APPLES

Earthy wild mushrooms and tart green apples are a surprisingly good combination. Here they mingle in a sinfully delicious Madeira and mascarpone sauce which takes literally minutes to prepare. Try it as a topping for crostini, a filling for pancakes, or as follows, a warm salad on top of a few crisp leaves.

> **400g/14 oz. mixed wild mushrooms, especially chanterelles and ceps, cleaned and sliced if large, or a mixture of cultivated and wild**
> **2 Granny Smith apples, peeled, cored, sliced and dressed with a squeeze of lemon**
> **1 glass of Madeira wine**
> **150g / 5 oz. mascarpone cheese**
> **30g / 1 oz. butter**
> **salt and pepper**
> **sweet, crisp lettuce such as cos, oak leaf, little gem, washed and dried**

Melt the butter on moderate heat in a wide frying pan and add the mushrooms with a sprinkling of salt and pepper. When they have absorbed the butter and begin to soften, add the apples and sauté for 2 or 3 minutes. Pour in the Madeira and cook, stirring, until it has mostly evaporated and the juices begin to caramelise. Finally, stir in the mascarpone. Allow it to melt and coat everything with its sweet creaminess.

Arrange lettuce on four plates, and spoon over the warm mushroom mixture. Eat right away.

SERVES 4

SIMPLE VEGETABLES

CREAMED BEETROOT GREENS

It astonishes me that many vegetable vendors and cooks throw away the luscious greens of the beetroot. They are the best green since chard, sweet and not gritty or bitter, and you may find they are the cheapest, as well, coming free with the beetroot. A veg man in Wales once insisted I was a savage when I relieved him of an enormous box of beetroot greens destined for the rubbish bin. It's always worth asking in the market if they have some stashed away. I think they taste best when treated these two ways.

Brown some chopped onion in butter in a lidded pot. Add some chopped garlic and sauté until fragrant. Add washed, chopped beetroot greens, stir and cover. Cook for 3-5 minutes, stirring now and then, until just wilted. They will reduce to about a third of their original volume.

Or serve them in a bright pink, creamy sauce by following the same method and adding a tablespoon of plain flour after the garlic. Cook for a couple of minutes, stirring, and pour in some milk to make a roux. When the sauce thickens, add the beetroot greens, cover and cook until wilted.

LAVISH LEEKS IN MANDARIN SAUCE

Purchasing leeks can seem like an extravagance, since often the bulk of the weight, in the green tops, is too tough to eat. Buy them in season (August to April) and when possible, trimmed. Now freshly squeezed mandarin juice really is an extravagance, though orange juice will suffice. Saffron is nearly worth its weight in gold at several hundred pounds per pound, but you only need a pinch. Serve leeks this way as a side vegetable or as a delicious neon orange sauce for anything bland or delicate.

Slice about a pound (500g) of leeks quite thinly. Sauté gently in a generous knob of melted butter (60 g / 2 oz.) until soft and just beginning to colour. Sprinkle in a tablespoon of plain flour and cook for a couple of minutes, stirring. Gradually add 200 ml / 7 fl. oz. freshly squeezed mandarin or orange juice with a pinch of saffron filaments. Season well with salt and pepper. Stir while the sauce thickens. Best served right away.

MEXICAN CUCUMBERS

In Mexico, you would find these served as a free snack at the bar alongside your *cerveza*. They taste alarmingly delicious, and contain virtually no calories. "Mild Chilli Powder" is a common mixture of ground chilli, cumin, salt, garlic and oregano. It is essential to the flavour here, and is a good all-purpose Mexican seasoning to have on the shelf anyway. A hot version is available, but it is designed for asbestos palates.

1 medium cucumber
2 limes
mild chilli powder
salt

Cut the cucumber across into four pieces of equal length. Cut each piece into four lengths. Arrange the pieces skin-side-down in a dish and squeeze the lime juice over them. Sprinkle with an even coat of mild chilli powder and a bit of salt.

They are best eaten with your fingers, chased down with a cold lager.

SOUTHERN FRIED OKRA

Okra is undeniably slimy. This makes it a profoundly unpopular vegetable in this part of the world. But its very sliminess renders it ideal for coating, as it acts like an egg white. My Texan mother snatched up young okra from the farmer's market at every available opportunity to prepare it in the following manner, and it is sure to convert even the staunchest okra-hater.

Large or old okra will be tough, so buy fresh and small. Buy more than you think you can eat, as it shrinks significantly when cooked. Cut crosswise into 1 cm / ½ inch pieces. Put a few table-spoons of polenta (cornmeal) in a plastic bag and season well with salt and pepper. Chuck in the okra pieces and shake the bag so that each piece is well coated.

Heat a shallow pool of olive or vegetable oil in a frying pan over moderate heat. Add the coated okra and fry, turning occasionally, until very crisp and golden. Drain on kitchen paper and devour!

GARLIC-SCENTED ROASTED BUTTERNUT SQUASH

This method can be used for any squash, but butternut is my favourite. Its name describes it well. It is hard and pear-shaped, its flesh velvety, nutty, sweet and deep yellow. It looks and tastes beautiful. One butternut will serve 2-4 people.

Preheat the oven to its highest setting. Slice the squash in half from stem to base. Scoop the seeds out with a spoon and lay the squash on a baking sheet, skin side down. Place two whole cloves of garlic in each round cavity. Pour about two teaspoons of olive oil over the garlic and, using a pastry brush, paint the oil all over the surface of the flesh. Bake for 30-40 minutes, until tender and lightly browned around the edges.

The flesh around the cavity will have taken on a delicate garlic flavour. The garlic itself will be soft and its strength tamed. Eat the garlic as it is or mash with a pinch of coarse salt and spread on bread.

PARSNIP CRISPS

These toothsome morsels hardly resemble parsnips at all. They are best nibbled out of a bowl with a little dish of runny honey for dipping. Try the same procedure with beetroot, carrot, sweet potato...

2 fat parsnips
60g / 2 oz. butter, melted
salt

Preheat the oven to 120°C / 250°F / Gas ½. Trim the ends of the parsnips, peel and patiently slice into the thinnest discs you can manage. Lay them in a large baking dish and pour the butter over them. Toss to coat evenly. Sprinkle with salt. Bake for one hour, giving them a good stir and shake every 10-15 minutes, to dry them out and prevent burning. They should be dark golden and crispy when done.

STUFFED FAVOURITES

POTATO AND ROASTED GARLIC FILO PARCELS

I created this filling for filo parcels when I had to meet criteria for a buffet which was staggered over several hours. They won't go soggy and taste just as good cold as hot. Once you get the hang of the rolling you can make hundreds if necessary, and very inexpensively. As a light meal, they go brilliantly with *Sesame Sauce* (p.88) and some raw celery, radishes, red peppers, cucumber and cherry tomatoes. Perfect for a picnic.

**1 whole bulb of garlic
olive oil
1 kg / 2 lb. potatoes
200g / 7 oz. Feta cheese, crumbled
100g / 3 ½ oz. black olives, pitted
juice and grated zest of 1 lemon
1 Tbsp. coriander seeds, crushed
salt and pepper to taste
10-12 sheets of filo pastry, each measuring
 approximately 30cm / 12 inches by 17cm /
 7 inches (the filo can be cut to this size, just
 slightly thinner than an A4 piece of paper)
125g / 4 oz. butter, melted
50g / 2 oz. sesame seeds**

Preheat the oven to 150°C / 300°F / Gas 2.

Cut the bulb of garlic in half equatorially, that is, through each clove rather than head to root. Brush with olive oil and slow-roast for about a half an hour, until golden.

Boil the potatoes until quite soft, then mash, leaving some texture. Squeeze the garlic out of its skin and mash to a paste. Add to the potatoes with the Feta, lemon essences, olives and coriander. Mix well, incorporating everything evenly. Taste and season with salt and plenty of pepper.

Preheat the oven to 180°C / 350°F / Gas 4. Unroll your pastry sheets and cover with a moist, clean tea towel to prevent them drying out. Take one sheet and brush with melted butter. Fold in half to form a long thin rectangle. Brush again with butter, turn over and brush again. Take about a handful of potato mixture and place in the bottom right corner of the sheet. Shape the mixture into a rough triangle, with the right angle matching the pastry corner. Lift the pastry from the same corner and flop it up and over, so the corner meets the opposite edge. Flop it over again towards the top of the sheet, and carry on until you reach the top. Seal any loose pastry with your buttery fingers. Place the parcels on a greased baking sheet and sprinkle with sesame seeds. Bake for 30 minutes, until deep golden.

MAKES 10-12

RED LENTIL AND CARAMELISED ONION CABBAGE PARCELS

The idea of cabbage with lentils may not send an electrocuting jolt of inspiration through your veins; it is redolent of the bad vegetarian food of yore. But if you open your mind and your taste buds to this marvellously simple dish, you will fall back in love with its humble ingredients. Savoy cabbage leaves, beautifully veiny and fibrous, encapsulate a soft, lemony filling offset by the luxurious sweetness of caramelised onions—no fancy spices are necessary. These tender, salubrious parcels hold their own, though a rich tomato sauce (see *Red Ginger Coulis* p.55) is the ideal companion, along with some rice and a generous dollop of Greek yoghurt. The recipe can easily be multiplied to feed the masses.

1 savoy cabbage
200 g / 7 oz. red lentils
3 large onions, halved and sliced
1 Tbsp. olive oil
2 tsp. sugar
grated zest and juice of one large lemon
salt and freshly ground black pepper
olive oil or melted butter

Put a large pot of salted water on to boil.

Wash the lentils, place them in a small lidded saucepan and cover with cold water. Bring to the boil and skim off the foam. Let them boil rapidly for ten minutes, stirring from time to time, then reduce the heat to a simmer, add some salt and cover. You may need to add a bit more water if they seem to be drying out. Simmer for about 15 minutes, stirring and checking that they're not burning on the bottom. The resulting consistency should be like porridge.

Meanwhile, cut the cabbage leaves carefully away from the core, discarding the outermost leaves if they look tough. Shave down any particularly thick stems. Blanch in the boiling pot for two minutes only, then refresh in cold water and leave to drain. (Use the blanching water to cook rice if you are doing so.)

Sauté the onions with the olive oil on moderate heat. When they start to go brown, add the sugar. Stir them attentively until nicely caramelised.

Combine the onions, cooked lentils, lemon juice and zest. Taste it—you may wish to add more salt. Grind in some pepper. Preheat the oven to 180°C / 350°F / Gas 4.

Pat dry a cabbage leaf. Place a heaped spoonful of filling in the middle near the base of the leaf. Fold over the sides, then roll it up. Place seam-side down in a greased baking dish. Brush lightly with olive oil or, even better, melted butter. Bake for 20-25 minutes until lightly browned. Serve hot, warm, or cold.

MAKES 10-12 PARCELS

STUFFED FLAT MUSHROOMS WITH HERBED YOGHURT CUSTARD

Flat, open mushrooms sing out to be filled and roasted. Here their gilled craters enclose round companions tomato and onion in a pool of bright yellow custard.

4 large flat mushrooms, stalks removed
4 slices beefsteak tomato
4 slices large white onion
1 Tbsp. chopped fresh rosemary
2 cloves of garlic, chopped
4 Tbsp. olive oil
salt and pepper
200 g / 7 oz. Greek yoghurt
2 egg yolks
small handful each of basil and chives, chopped
30 g / 1 oz. freshly grated Parmesan

Preheat the oven to 180°C / 350°F / Gas 4.

Place the mushrooms on a baking sheet and arrange the onion and tomato slices inside the cavities. Mix together the olive oil, rosemary and garlic and spoon into the mushrooms. Season with salt and pepper.

Combine the yoghurt, egg yolks, basil, chives, and Parmesan and whisk together thoroughly. Season with salt and pepper. Spoon into each mushroom cavity; don't worry if some spills over the edge.

Bake in the oven for 15-20 minutes until the custard has set.
Eat right away.

**SERVES 4 AS A STARTER
OR ACCOMPANIMENT**

NEW PIEDMONTESE PEPPERS

Elizabeth David first brought these our way in her *Italian Food*. Forty years later, Delia Smith penetrated nearly every British household with her version. Here's yet another. There is simply no better way to stuff peppers, so they act as a miniature roasting dish, stewing up the tomatoes and basil in garlicky juices. I've replaced anchovies with olives and capers, which add a subtle flavour and glisten like jewels. Choose tomatoes which will fit inside the peppers. It is not absolutely necessary to skin the tomatoes, but it is a simple enough procedure which makes the whole thing more elegant. Use yellow or orange peppers as well as red. Green are nice, too, but have quite a different flavour.

4 red peppers
4 ripe tomatoes
4 cloves of garlic, sliced
16 black olives
2 Tbsp. capers
16 large basil leaves
8 Tbsp. olive oil
8 tsp. balsamic vinegar
salt and pepper

Preheat the oven to 200°C / 400°F / Gas 6. Cut the peppers in half from stem to base. Carefully cut away the seeds, but leave just the stem intact. This will help them hold their shape. Lay the peppers in a roasting dish.

Skin the tomatoes. Place them in a bowl and pour boiling water over them. Leave for a minute and drain. When cool enough to handle, slip the skins off with the assistance of a paring knife if necessary. Cut out any tough bits and quarter into wedges.

Place two tomato quarters in each pepper half. Tuck a few garlic slices into each. Tear the basil and tuck in, plus two olives each and a few capers. Follow with a tablespoon of olive oil, a teaspoon of balsamic vinegar, and season generously with salt and pepper.

Roast the peppers for 30 minutes or until they are starting to blacken around the edges. Eat hot, warm or cold, with bread.

**SERVES 8 AS A STARTER OR ACCOMPANIMENT,
OR 4 GREEDY PEOPLE**

STUFFED BUNS

The pizza dough recipe I use at home makes a batch large enough for about three large pizzas, so it can last through the week for a few meals. These little stuffed globes are a convenient snack made in minutes by grabbing a couple of handfuls of dough out of the fridge and a bit of imagination. Left over ratatouille, pesto or a lump of melting cheese also make good fillings. If you lack the confidence or amusement for making yeasted dough, buy a tube of ready-to-bake dough or make some up from a packet of dough mix for a yummy, portable snack, hot or cold.

300 g / 10 oz. dough
100 g / 3 ½ oz. cream cheese
10 g / 1/3 oz. dried porcini (cep) mushrooms
a handful of snipped chives
1 egg, beaten
freshly ground pepper

Pour boiling water over the mushrooms and leave for 20 minutes. Preheat the oven to 200°C / 400°F / Gas 6.

Chop the rehydrated mushrooms and mash together with the cream cheese, chives and pepper.

Divide the dough into eight equal parts. Flatten and stretch a piece into a pancake and place a tablespoon of stuffing in the middle. Wrap the dough around the filling and pinch firmly to seal all escape routes. Place each bun seam-side-down on a lightly greased baking sheet. Gloss each bun with beaten egg.

Bake for 15-20 minutes, until puffed and golden.

FOR 8 BUNS

FRENCH TOAST ROLLS

ingers of good melting cheese work well as a filling for these, but you can use anything you might stuff an omelette with, as they're a bit of an omelette/French toast hybrid. For a sweet version, you could try some soft fruit or jam in the middle with a little crème fraîche, and add sugar to the egg rather than thyme. The most suitable bread for the job is a good quality white square-tin sandwich loaf, medium sliced. Sorry, it's not the healthiest of recipes. It's sheer wickedness.

8 slices white sandwich bread
4 eggs
75 ml / 2 ½ fl. oz. milk
salt and pepper
leaves stripped from a few thyme sprigs,
125 g / 4 oz. melting cheese such as Cheddar,
**   Gruyère or Havarti**
100 g / 3 ½ oz. butter

Slice the crusts off the bread. In a wide bowl, whisk together the eggs, milk and thyme and season. Cut the cheese into eight equal rod-shaped pieces.

To construct each roll, place a finger of cheese at the top of a slice of bread and roll up tightly. Moisten your fingertips in a cup of water and rub across the seam to seal. Coat the rolls in the egg mixture and leave them to soak in it for ten minutes.

Melt the butter in a frying pan and cook the rolls over low to moderate heat, turning frequently to cook evenly on all sides. When they are deep golden all over and the cheese begins to ooze out, it's time to eat.

FOR 8 SMALL ROLLS

MAJOR DISHES

CELEBRATION PIE WITH RED GINGER COULIS

I thought this pie through and invented it on my wedding day, which was a great celebration. It was a small wedding, and I had lots of family help with the cooking. The pie went down very well and I've had many requests for the recipe, so here it is, after multitudinous attempts at recreating it. It's ideal for Christmas dinner, but the asparagus layer in the middle may not suit a winter celebration. Substitute cooked spinach or something else green.

For the pie:
3 Tbsp. olive oil
250 g / 8 oz. mushrooms, sliced
2 medium onions, chopped
1 red pepper, chopped
4 cloves of garlic, chopped
1 Tbsp. fresh thyme leaves
¼ a whole nutmeg, grated
100 g / 3 ½ oz. pine nuts
grated zest and juice of one lemon
125 g / 4 oz. dry white breadcrumbs
125 g / fresh grated Parmesan
3 eggs, beaten
250 g / 8 oz. asparagus, preferably fine, lightly cooked
5 large or 10 small leaves filo pastry, defrosted if frozen
100 g / 3 ½ oz. butter, melted
salt and pepper

For the red ginger coulis:
150 ml / 5 fl oz. olive oil
4-5 cloves of garlic, chopped
2 walnut-size pieces of ginger, chopped
2 x 400g / 14 oz. tins chopped tomatoes
1 Tbsp. balsamic vinegar

1 Tbsp. dark brown sugar
150 ml / 5 fl. oz. Madeira wine
salt, pepper and cayenne pepper to taste

To make the pie, heat the olive oil in a frying pan over a moderately high flame. Fry the mushrooms with salt, and grind pepper into them until your wrist aches. Cook until most of the moisture has evaporated. Add the onions and red pepper and cook until they start to colour. Add the garlic and enjoy the fragrance for a minute or two, then remove from the heat. Transfer to a bowl and mix in the thyme, nutmeg and lemon essences. Let it cool down a bit and purée in the food processor so that it is well minced but not like baby food. Combine the mixture with breadcrumbs, pine nuts, 100 g / 3 ½ oz. of the Parmesan and the eggs. Preheat the oven to 200°C / 400°F / Gas 6.

Brush a 24 cm / 9 fi inch springform cake tin with melted butter. Moisten a clean tea towel and use it to cover the filo pastry and stop it drying out while you work. Layer one pastry leaf inside the tin and brush all over with melted butter. Keep layering and buttering to line the entire tin, leaving no gaps.

Spoon half of the filling into the case. Arrange the asparagus in a row, covering as much of the surface as possible. Add the remaining filling and smooth it down. Fold down the surplus pastry over the top. If the filling is not completely covered, add another leaf of buttered pastry. Butter the top of the pie and sprinkle with the remaining Parmesan.

Place on a baking sheet and bake for 20 minutes. Take it out of the oven and remove the springform by standing the pie on an upturned bowl. Slide it off the base and back onto the baking sheet. Bake for a further 15 minutes, until crisp and golden. Cool for 5-10 minutes before slicing into wedges and serve with Red Ginger Coulis.

To make the coulis, heat the olive oil in a saucepan and add the garlic and ginger. Fry until fragrant, then add the rest of the ingredients. Simmer gently for 20-30 minutes, stirring frequently. Taste for seasoning.

Remove the pan from the heat and, after a few minutes, purée with a hand blender. For an elegant consistency, push the sauce through a sieve. Reheat gently and serve.

SERVES 6-8

CABBAGE GATEAU

This technique of layering and pressing cabbage leaves opens up infinite possibilities for fillings. In this version, little bursts of flavour from the toasted seeds and smoky bacon bits are launched by the sweet marmalade and salty cheese. This creates a complex taste sensation out of simplicity itself.

1 large cabbage, preferably Savoy
3 Tbsp. marmalade
50g / 2 oz. sesame seeds, toasted in a dry frying pan
1 Tbsp. caraway seeds, toasted in a dry frying pan
50g / 2 oz. vegetarian bacon bits (optional)
200g / 7 oz. assorted hard cheeses such as mature Cheddar, Gruyère, and Gouda, grated

Bring a large pot of water to the boil and salt it well. Carefully cut about 16 cabbage leaves away from the core. Shave off any tough stems and wash thoroughly. Have a bowl of iced water ready next to the pot. Boil the leaves for 3 minutes, then plunge into iced water.

Drain the cabbage well. Lightly grease a large oven-proof plate. Pat dry one cabbage leaf and place in the centre of the plate. Brush lightly with marmalade, then sprinkle with seeds. Place another dry leaf on top, brush with marmalade, and sprinkle with one type of cheese and bacon bits. Continue layering alternately (small leaves can be overlapped) and finish with a cabbage leaf, reserving a little cheese. Trim the edges and arrange the excess evenly on top of the gâteau.

Place another plate on top and weigh it down with a heavy book or something similar. Leave it for at least half an hour, then drain off excess moisture. Preheat the oven to 200°C / 400°F / Gas 6.

Finally, remove the top plate carefully and sprinkle the remaining cheese on top. Pop it in the oven for 20 minutes, until thoroughly heated and browned on top. Allow to cool down just a little, then cut into wedges. You may wish to transfer to another plate to serve.

SERVES 4

MIX AND MATCH RICH BUT FAT-FREE VEGETABLE HOT POT

This dish is always a hit, but I'm never certain which combination of vegetables and legumes is the best. The absolutely consistent ingredient is the carrot juice, which can be fresh or long-life. It is simply poured over the vegetables and seasonings and simmered in the oven, producing a very richly flavoured, dazzling stew, without oil or fat. A small bowl-full with some bread makes a hearty meal. It can also be served with couscous or rice. The vegetables listed are guidelines only: just fill up your best deep roasting dish or casserole with roots, peppers, mushrooms, beans and something green, add the herbs, spices and seasonings, pour over the carrot juice, and bake. After just over an hour your oven will reveal a fascinatingly good concoction.

The vegetables:
250 g / 8 oz. celeriac
250 g / 8 oz. sweet potato
2 red onions
1 red pepper
100 g / 3 ½ oz. shiitake mushrooms
200 g / 7 oz. tomatoes
100 g / 3 ½ oz. runner beans
**1 x 400 g / 14 oz. tin chick peas, drained and
   rinsed**

The rest:
4 cloves of garlic, chopped
finely grated rind of 1 lemon
handful of chopped basil and parsley
1 tsp. coriander seeds, freshly ground
a good grinding of nutmeg
salt, pepper and cayenne to taste
1 litre / 1 ¾ pints carrot juice
yoghurt and chopped herbs to serve

Preheat the oven to 180°C / 350°F / Gas 4. Cut up all the

vegetables into chunky bite-size pieces. Place in a deep roasting or casserole dish. Sprinkle over the rest of the ingredients and pour in the juice. Stir. Cover with foil and bake in the oven for 45 minutes. Remove the foil and stir again. Reduce the temperature to 150°C / 300°F / Gas 2 and bake uncovered for another half an hour to let the juices thicken. Serve from the dish into warmed bowls. Garnish with a dollop of yoghurt and some more chopped herbs, if desired.

SERVES 4-6

CRISP TERIYAKI BEAN CURD WITH SOBA NOODLES

I cannot claim that this is an authentic Japanese dish; it has been rather naturalised. Japanese cuisine is beautifully minimalist; this is something you can really sink your teeth into. But the flavour is authentic. Two uniquely Japanese ingredients, sake and mirin, reduced with soy sauce, form what I call the "holy trinity" of Japanese flavour, or teriyaki, which actually means "shining grill". Bean curd simmered in this divine liquor and fried crisp could, dare I say, outshine a steak to meat lovers. In any case, it's a vegetarian's dream.

For the bean curd:
150 ml / 5 fl oz. sake (Japanese wine)
150 ml / 5 fl oz. mirin (Japanese cooking wine—somewhat sweeter)
150 ml / 5 fl oz. dark soy sauce
125 g / 4 oz. shiitake mushrooms, stems removed and sliced
500 g / 1 lb. fresh bean curd (tofu)
4 Tbsp. cornflour
1 tsp. ground ginger
large pinch cayenne pepper or to taste oil for frying

For the noodles:
200 g / 7 oz. mange tout, trimmed
200 g / 7 oz. soba (buckwheat) noodles
1 bunch spring onions, thinly sliced
1 red pepper, sliced into thin matchsticks
4 handfuls of rocket, washed and dried
2 Tbsp. sesame seeds, toasted
sprigs of coriander to garnish

Make the teriyaki marinade. Combine the sake, mirin, soy sauce and sliced mushrooms in a wide saucepan and bring to the boil.

Simmer gently for 15 minutes. Meanwhile, drain the bean curd and dry slightly with paper towels. Cut into eight triangles. Poach the bean curd in the simmered marinade for 10 minutes, turning over once during cooking. Remove carefully with a slotted spoon and take the marinade off the heat.

Prepare the noodles. Bring a pot of water to the boil and blanch the mange tout for 30 seconds. Remove the mange tout and cool them under cold running water. Add the noodles to the pot. Bring back to the boil and cook, stirring gently, for 4-5 minutes, until tender. Drain the noodles and run cold water over them until cool. Drain well and mix with the mange tout, spring onions and red pepper. This is most efficiently done with clean hands. Set aside.

On a plate, combine the cornflour, ginger and cayenne. Coat the bean curd all over with this mixture. Heat a shallow pool of oil in a pan. Fry the bean curd on all sides until crisp and deep golden. Drain on paper towels.

Place a handful of rocket on each plate. Next a nest of noodles. Crown with two pieces of bean curd, spoon teriyaki sauce and mushrooms over each heap, and sprinkle with sesame seeds. Sprigs of coriander to decorate.

SERVES 4

CASSEROLE TRICOLORE

This visual stunner, a collage of Mediterranean vegetables, is a delight to deliver to the dinner table, and tastes even more spectacular. Tricolore refers to its three colours, red, green and gold. It is an extremely juicy dish and makes a divine light meal with lots of crusty bread. Leftovers are awfully nice cold as a roasted vegetable salad.

The vegetables:
1 red pepper, cut in long strips
500 g / 1 lb. plum tomatoes, skinned and
    quartered
3 courgettes, sliced in 1 cm / ½ inch discs
1 x 400g / 14 oz. tin artichoke hearts, drained
    and halved
1 medium aubergine, sliced in 0.5 cm / ¼ inch
    discs
1 large onion, roughly the same circumference as
    the aubergine, sliced to the same thickness

The dressing:
4 Tbsp. olive oil
2 Tbsp. balsamic vinegar
4 cloves of garlic, finely sliced
a handful of fresh basil, shredded
2 Tbsp. capers
1 tsp. salt, or to taste

a handful of black olives and fresh bay leaves to
    decorate
salt and freshly ground black pepper

Preheat the oven to its highest setting. Lightly grease a wide oblong roasting dish. The arrangement of the vegetables in the dish makes it the *pièce de résistance*. Place the red pepper and tomatoes in one stripe across the top of the dish and the courgette and artichoke hearts similarly across the bottom. Arrange the slices of aubergine and onion interleaved with one another in the middle.

Whisk together the dressing ingredients and spoon over the vegetables as evenly as possible. Keep back a little bit and paint it on with a pastry brush to cover every exposed surface. Season with lots of pepper and decorate with olives and bay leaves.

Roast for 45 minutes to an hour, until well-browned around the edges.

SERVES 8

GRILLED POLENTA AND AUBERGINE STACKS WITH BEETROOT SALSA

This is a colourful and impressive summertime dish which is quick to make once the polenta is cooked and cooled. Save a couple of 400 g / 14 oz. food tins and use them as moulds for the polenta. It can then be cooled and sliced into neat little rounds which are stacked with the vegetables in between. Alternatively, you can spread the polenta on a flat board before cooling, and then cut out rounds or squares. Choose aubergines, onions and tomatoes which have a similar circumference.

For the stacks:
1.75 litres / 3 pints water
275g / 9 oz. coarse-grained yellow cornmeal
1 Tbsp. salt
2 aubergines, sliced into eight 1 cm/ ½ inch rounds
2 large onions, sliced into eight 0.5 cm/ ¼ inch rounds
2 beefsteak tomatoes, sliced into eight 1 cm / ½ inch rounds
olive oil
a few drops of balsamic vinegar
salt and pepper
grated fresh Parmesan and rocket leaves to decorate

For the salsa:
4 beetroots
juice of 2 lemons
remaining onion and tomato, finely chopped
a handful of chopped coriander
a handful of chopped parsley
a pinch of sugar
salt and pepper

First make the polenta. Boil the water in a large, heavy pot, add the salt, and sprinkle in the cornmeal a handful at a time, stirring constantly with a wooden spoon. On medium heat, keep stirring for 30-40 minutes, until the polenta pulls away easily from the sides of the pot.

Pour into the cling film-lined cylinder, or smooth out the polenta onto a flat tray or board which has been moistened with water, to a 1 cm / ½ inch thickness. Allow to cool completely. Refrigerate overnight if desired.

Make the salsa. Scrub the beetroots and boil for about 30 minutes, until tender. Drain and rub off the skins under cool running water. Chop finely and combine in a bowl with the rest of the salsa ingredients. Set aside.

Preheat the oven to 200°C / 400°F / Gas 6.

Arrange the onion rounds on an oiled baking tray, brush with oil and season. Top each slice with an aubergine round, brush with oil and season. Bake for 30 minutes or until the aubergines are nicely browned on top.

Meanwhile, slip the polenta out of the cylinder and slice into 16 rounds. Or cut 16 7.5cm / 3 inch rounds out of the slab with a pastry cutter or drinking glass. (You can make delicious fried croutons with the trimmings!) If all of this seems too complicated, just cut the polenta into 16 squares. Arrange them on an oiled baking tray which will fit under the grill.

Once the aubergines are cooked, preheat the grill. Brush the polenta slices with olive oil and grill until lightly browned. Keep warm.

Place the tomato slices on top of the aubergines, drizzle with olive oil and balsamic vinegar, and season. Place under the grill for a couple of minutes until sizzling.

Now assemble the stacks. On each plate, place two polenta slices side by side. Top each with a stack of vegetables, and then another slice of polenta. Sprinkle with Parmesan.

If desired, pour the cooking juices from the vegetable pan into the bowl of salsa and stir. Spoon the salsa generously onto the stacks. Surround with a few rocket leaves and serve.

SERVES 4-6

VARIATIONS ON CLASSICS

MEXICAN GAZPACHO

The addition of avocado, lime and spice transports the classic Spanish soup back to the New World, where its tomato base originated. It's hard to beat on a hot summer day for refreshment. Chill the soup fast by placing it in the freezer, stirring from time to time. A few ice crystals melting quickly on the tongue is an exciting sensation. If you have the foresight, make a garnish of ice cubes with a single coriander leaf frozen inside.

**2 cloves garlic
coarse salt and pepper
1 cucumber
1 yellow pepper
2 celery stalks
4 ripe tomatoes
1 red onion
1 litre / 1 ¾ pints fresh tomato pressé or tomato
    juice
2 tsp. cumin seeds, toasted in a dry frying pan
1 tsp. mild chilli powder
1 ripe avocado
juice of 2 limes**

To serve:
**coriander and / or coriander ice cubes
crème fraîche or Greek yoghurt**

In a mortar, mash up the garlic with the salt until fairly smooth. Coarsely chop the cucumber, pepper, celery, tomatoes and onion and mix together in a bowl with the garlic. Place half of the vegetables in a food processor and purée until smooth-ish. Transfer to a large bowl. Process the other half of the vegetables using the pulse button until well chopped but still a little chunky. Add to the purée. Stir in the tomato juice and spices. Taste for seasoning, adding more salt and pepper as necessary. Cut the

70

avocado into little cubes and dress with the lime juice. Stir into the gazpacho.

Chill for several hours or overnight. If desired, place the soup in the freezer for half an hour before serving to get it especially cold. Serve each bowl with a dollop of crème fraîche or Greek yoghurt plus a couple of coriander ice cubes, or chopped coriander sprinkled on top.

SERVES 6

BORSCHT WITH HOT NEW POTATOES AND DILL CREAM

There are hundreds of recipes for this popular Lithuanian export. My version is particularly low on labour, very clean-tasting and is a spectacle of magenta, white and green. Though the soup is traditionally served cold, and eaten in summer when beetroots are best, I think it is equally good served hot. In either case, the potatoes should be just boiled and still warm. This is another fat-free recipe, if you leave out the dill cream. Low-fat yoghurt or fromage frais could be substituted for crème fraîche.

For the soup:
800g / 1 ½ lbs. fresh beetroot
1 small onion or ½ a large one, coarsely chopped
juice and grated zest of 1 lemon
1 tsp. whole cloves, freshly ground, or ¼ tsp. pre-ground
500ml / 16 fl. oz. apple juice, preferably fresh pressed
750ml / 1 ¼ pints vegetable stock
salt and pepper to taste

For the dill cream:
250ml / 8 fl. oz. crème fraîche
1 handful of dill, chopped or snipped with scissors

To serve:
24 hot baby new potatoes
1 handful of chives, chopped or snipped with scissors

Bring a large pot of water to the boil and salt it well. Trim the leaves off, if any, (see *Creamed Beetroot Greens* p.37) but try not to puncture the skin or much of its bold pink juice will bleed out while cooking. Scrub the beetroots and boil for 30-40 minutes, until tender. Drain and rinse in cold water and rub off the skins, tops and spindly roots. Chop coarsely.

In the blender, place one beetroot, the onion, lemon essences, cloves, and some salt and pepper. Purée until smooth.

In the rinsed-out boiling pot, place the cooked beetroot, beetroot purée, apple juice and stock. Bring to the boil and simmer gently for 15 minutes. Meanwhile, cook the potatoes and prepare the dill cream by mixing the dill and crème fraîche together.

When the soup is cooked, cool briefly and then purée.

Leave the soup to cool completely and refrigerate for several hours, or serve hot, with three potatoes in each bowl, a generous blob of dill cream and a sprinkling of chives.

SERVES 8

SLOW-ROASTED TOMATO TART

This is the *Universal Fruit Tart* (p.106) in a savoury form, and tomatoes are a fruit, after all. We are witnessing a bit of a comeback of the savoury tart, after a couple of decades of badly made quiches nearly extinguished the delectable lunch dish all together. The quiche is dead...long live the savoury tart!

2 kg / 4 lbs. ripe plum tomatoes
6 cloves of garlic, finely sliced
4 Tbsp. olive oil
2 Tbsp. balsamic vinegar
salt and pepper
a little sugar
3 egg yolks
1 egg white
150 g / 5 oz. crème fraîche
2 handfuls of basil leaves
1 savoury pastry base, baked blind (See *Notes* p.14)

Preheat the oven to 150°C / 300°F / Gas 2.

Place the tomatoes in a bowl and pour boiling water over them. Leave for a minute, then drain. When cool enough to handle, slip off the skins, using a small paring knife to assist you. Slice each tomato in half and place cut-side up in a roasting dish. Tuck a few slices of garlic into each tomato. Drizzle with olive oil and balsamic vinegar, and sprinkle with salt, pepper and a little sugar. Roast in the oven for 1-1 ½ hours, until shrunken and brown around the edges.

Increase the oven temperature to 180°C / 350°F / Gas 4. Brush the egg white over the bottom of the pastry case: this will prevent it from getting soggy. Arrange the tomatoes in the pastry case.

Add any remaining pan juices as well. Mix together the egg yolks and crème fraîche and tear in the basil leaves. Season with salt and pepper and mix well. Pour over the tomatoes and bake the tart for 30-40 minutes until the custard is set and lightly browned.

Let the tart stand for 5 minutes and remove the tin. Cut into wedges and eat right away with a rocket salad and balsamic vinaigrette.

SERVES 4

ONE-PAN EGGS FLORENTINE FOR TWO

This recipe was inspired by my husband, whose enjoyment of cooking is usually directly disproportionate to the amount of washing up inflicted by the process. The entire procedure requires only one heavy-bottomed, medium-sized pan, a shallow dish or bowl which fits snugly on top of it (as a *bain-marie*), a slotted spatula and a whisk (and of course two plates, cutlery, and a toaster). It simplifies a classic dish which usually demands several different techniques (and pots and pans), all of which have to be executed with precise timing. Sometimes the most rewarding and delicious meals are the simplest. There's something rather romantic about this one as well, especially as a lazy, late breakfast.

a little oil
400 ml / 14 fl. oz water
1 tsp. vinegar
salt
2 free-range eggs (or 4 if you're very hungry)
2 egg yolks
4 tsp. lemon juice
100 g / 3 ½ oz. salted butter, cubed, plus extra
    for the muffins
200 g / 7 oz. spinach, trimmed and washed
2 muffins, split

Heat the oven to 160°C / 325°F / Gas 3 and put a couple of plates in to warm. Smear the oil in the pan: this should prevent the eggs from sticking. Pour in the water, add the vinegar and salt, and bring to the boil, then reduce to a simmer. Carefully break the eggs into the water and poach for a few minutes, to the desired doneness. This can be determined by prodding the yolk with a fork. If anything they should be slightly undercooked, as they will sit in the oven briefly. Remove the eggs from the water

with a slotted spatula and keep warm on one of the plates.
A couple of paper towels underneath the eggs will absorb excess water.

Stuff the spinach into the pot and cover with the *bain-marie* dish.
Melt the butter in the dish. (This is a good time to toast your muffins, with only a couple of minutes cooking time to go.) Mix together the egg yolks and lemon juice, then pour this into the melted butter all at once. Whisk until the sauce thickens: it may appear to curdle, but it will emulsify if you continue whisking. As soon as a nicely smooth, thick and pale sauce is achieved, remove the dish from the pan.

By this time the spinach should be perfectly cooked. Quickly drain it and press out the excess moisture.

Butter the toasted muffins and divide between two warm plates. Top with spinach and poached egg. Give the sauce a final whisk as it may have started to separate. Pour over the eggs, and serve with a good grinding of pepper. Eat right away.

SERVES 2

AUBERGINE, RICOTTA AND SMOKED CHILLI PESTO TIMBALE

Timbale describes anything prepared in a small round mould. Aubergines lend themselves well to this format due to their long round shape. The usual treatment of aubergines in this way is to layer them with tomato sauce, mozzarella and Parmesan, an eternally good combination. Choose plump aubergines with roughly the same circumference as the ramekins, but remember that they shrink a lot when cooked.

This makes a lovely first course or main meal accompaniment, turned out onto individual plates and surrounded with a few rocket leaves.

3-4 large aubergines
3 large cloves of garlic, sliced
olive oil
250 g / 8 oz. ricotta
salt and pepper

For the pesto:
1 dried smoked chilli, rehydrated in hot water, deseeded and chopped
2 tsp. smoked paprika (if you can get your hands on it)
large bunch of basil
100 g / 3 ½ oz. pine nuts, lightly toasted
2 cloves of garlic
60 g /2 oz. grated fresh parmesan
6 Tbsp. olive oil

Preheat the oven to 190°C / 375°F / Gas 5.

Slice the aubergines into 1 cm / ½ inch thick discs. Mix the garlic with some olive oil in a cup and brush both sides of the aubergines. Place on a baking tray and distribute the sliced garlic on top. Season with salt and pepper and bake until golden,

20-30 minutes. Leave to cool.

Make the pesto by mincing everything up in the food processor, drizzling the olive oil in bit by bit. Taste for seasoning.

Brush 8 ramekins lightly with olive oil and place an aubergine slice in each one. Top with about a tablespoon of ricotta, a generous spoonful of pesto, then another aubergine slice. Continue with another layer of ricotta, pesto, then aubergine.

Place the ramekins on a baking tray and bake for 15-20 minutes until sizzling. Cool briefly before inverting onto warm plates.

FOR 8 TIMBALES

HALLOUMI FAJITAS

ajitas rose to fame in the eighties in Tex-Mex restaurants, and may have been done to death by now, but they are indisputably delicious. Usually made with beef or chicken, vegetarians have had to miss out on the richly piquant marinated stuffing for tortillas. The fleshy texture of Halloumi cheese, with its fabulous ability to be cooked without melting, makes it an ideal meat substitute. If left to stand too long, however, it loses its tenderness, so try to eat it soon after cooking. It's fun for each diner to construct his or her own fajitas, for a zesty, informal meal with a simple leaf salad.

The marinade:
2 cloves of garlic
1 Tbsp. coarse salt
4 limes, the zest of 2 and the juice of 4
a handful of coriander, chopped
½ tsp. oregano
½ tsp. hot chilli powder
1 tsp. cumin seeds
1 tsp. sugar
1 Tbsp. white wine vinegar
100 ml / 3 ½ fl. oz. dark rum
100 ml / 3 ½ fl. oz. olive oil

The fajitas:
2 red onions, halved and sliced into wedges
1 red pepper, cut into strips
1 yellow pepper, cut into strips
1 green pepper, cut into strips
1 medium / 2 small courgettes, quartered
    lengthways and cut into chunks
200 g / 7 oz. mushrooms, quartered
500 g / 1 lb. Halloumi cheese, sliced
8-10 large white flour tortillas
soured cream or Greek yoghurt to serve

Guacamole:

2 ripe avocados
juice of 1 lime
dash of Worcestershire sauce
dash of Tabasco
salt to taste

Salsa Fresca:
300 g / 10 oz. ripe tomatoes, finely chopped
1 small onion, finely minced
2 green chillies, deseeded and finely minced
juice of 2-3 limes
small handful of coriander, finely chopped
salt to taste

To make the marinade, mash the garlic with the coarse salt in a mortar. Whisk all ingredients together except the oil. Whisk in the oil in a slow and steady stream. Place the prepared vegetables in a bowl and the Halloumi slices on a plate. Spoon enough marinade over the Halloumi just to coat. Pour the rest of the marinade over the vegetables and stir well. Cover both and leave to marinate for at least an hour.

Meanwhile make the guacamole. Scoop the avocado flesh into a bowl, add the lime juice and mash with a fork until fairly smooth but still a little lumpy. Add the remaining seasonings and adjust piquancy, adding a little more of this or that as desired. Make the salsa by combining all ingredients in a bowl. Cover the guacamole and salsa and set aside to let the flavours get acquainted.

Preheat the oven to warm. About half an hour before you are ready to serve, wrap the stacked tortillas in foil and place in the oven, along with a lidded serving dish. Select a wide, ideally cast iron frying pan which will accommodate all the vegetables, keeping in mind that they will shrink. Heat the pan over a high flame until scorching. Tip in the vegetables and any juices. Cook, stirring occasionally, until all the juices have reduced and the vegetables begin to fry. Keep a closer eye on it now, stirring frequently, but allowing the vegetables to turn deep golden and slightly charred. When they are all nicely browned and caramelised, after about 15 minutes, remove them to the warm lidded dish.

Keep the pan off the heat and pour in the extra marinade off the Halloumi. Then lay the Halloumi slices in a single layer on the bottom. Return to a medium flame. When the juices have boiled away, the Halloumi will quickly start to brown on the bottom. Carefully turn over each slice and brown the other side. Unite them with the vegetables and serve immediately.

To construct a fajita, lay a warm tortilla on a plate and spoon some of the cooked mixture on one half. Top with guacamole, salsa, and a generous dollop of soured cream or Greek yoghurt. Fold the tortilla over the heap and dig in.

SERVES 4-6

ACCOMPANI-MENTS

ROASTED CHILLI PEPPER JAM

This variety of jam is profuse in the Southwestern US. I improvised my first batch when I picked up a whole box of green peppers with a few chillies thrown in at the end of the day at Portobello Market for £1.00. (You can score some extraordinary "panda box" bargains at 6 p.m. on a Saturday.) I managed to produce twelve jars of the stuff which I gave away as Christmas presents. I spent a total of £3.68, two leisurely-paced hours and a great deal of affection, plus I finally utilised a fraction of the saved jars which have colonised my cupboard. The jam is dark green flecked with red. It has a sweet and mellow roasted flavour followed by a mean chilli bite which kicks in after a second or two. It has a happy marriage with Cheddar or cream cheese, and can be used as you would any sweet chilli sauce.

The weight of the peppers once deseeded, roasted and skinned reduces by about a third, but this will vary. Once you have completed this process, weigh the peppers. You should match the weight of the prepared peppers with the same amount in weight of sugar with pectin.

3 kg / 7 lb. fresh green peppers
10 hot, fleshy red chillies: Scotch bonnets, if you
    dare (wear gloves when handling chillies — see
    Notes p.12)
2 kg / 4 lb. sugar with pectin
juice and grated zest of two limes

preserving jars
heavy-bottomed stainless steel preserving pan

Preheat the oven or grill to the highest setting. Put a saucer in the fridge for testing the jam later. Cut the green peppers in half from stem to base and remove the stem and seeds. Place cut-side-down on a baking sheet and grill or roast until blackened and blistered all over. Remove to a plastic bag or bowl, seal or cover and leave to sweat until cool enough to handle. Prepare the chillies in the same way, though you may wish to keep them separate from the green peppers, as they will ooze their fiery juice when cooked.

Turn the oven down or heat it up to 160°C / 325°F / Gas 3. You can sterilise the jam jars while you wait for the peppers to cool. First be sure both jars and lids are squeaky clean. If you're using rubber seals, they must be new. Stand the jars on a paper towel-lined baking sheet and place in the oven for 10 minutes. Pour boiling water over the lids (if separate) and rubber seals, if using.

Next skin the peppers and chop coarsely. Mince the roasted chillies. Combine the two and process to a pulp with a few little chunks remaining. The easiest method is to put the pepper meats into a large bowl and purée with a hand-blender.

Scoop the pepper pulp into the preserving pan. Add the sugar, lime juice and zest. Bring to the boil, stirring constantly. It should come to a rapturous boil, scaling the walls of the pot in an eruption of glossy bubbles. Keep stirring it down and let it rage on for four minutes. Turn down the heat and test it on your chilled saucer—a few drops should form a wrinkly skin on top if it has set. If not, boil a bit longer. If it still doesn't set, try adding more lime juice. If it still doesn't set, don't worry. It will be a delicious sauce anyway.

Let it stand and settle for a few minutes, then ladle the hot jam carefully into the warm jars, leaving a little space. Attach the lids tightly and turn the jars upside-down once for a final seal. Use when cool or within two years.

MAKES ABOUT 1.75 LITRES / 3 PINTS OF JAM

RAW THAI SALSA

As a chilli addict, I think a lively hot salsa should be present at nearly every meal. In this one, the chilli should not dominate the subtle perfume of lime leaves and lemon grass. But the level of chilli intensity is a matter of personal taste. This peach-coloured salsa adds exotic flare to anything from rice and noodles to soups.

2 sticks fresh lemon grass, finely sliced
8 fresh lime leaves, hard middle stem discarded
   and very finely chopped
1 red chilli, sliced
1 garlic clove
juice of 1 lime
½ small onion
salt to taste
500 g /1 lb. ripe tomatoes
1 green pepper, chopped
1 medium carrot, peeled and grated

Cut the tomatoes in half and scoop the seeds out with a teaspoon. (This is important or else the salsa will be watery.)

Place one tomato in the blender with everything else except the green pepper and carrot. Whizz until completely smooth (1-2 minutes).

Chop the remaining tomatoes and add to the blender with the pepper and carrot. Pulse four times. Pour into a bowl and let the flavours get acquainted for a half hour or so before serving.

FETA AND LIME RELISH

S trong, salty Feta cheese mashed with these brash, zesty spices makes a sensational crowning dollop on a plate of couscous with a ragout of Mediterranean vegetables (try it with *Casserole Tricolore* p.64), as a stuffing for tomatoes or courgettes, or worked into a Greek salad with a twist. Earthy roasted root vegetables or lentils enjoy its company on the side. Infinite variations on the theme are possible with lemons or oranges, cumin, mint...I prefer to use French or Danish Feta as it has a creamier and less watery texture; proper Greek Feta sometimes has an offending "animal" taint, from the ewe's milk.

400g / 14 oz. Feta cheese
juice and grated zest of 2 limes
1 Tbsp. coriander seeds, toasted in a dry frying
    pan, and crushed in a mortar
a handful of coriander, chopped
1 or 2 hot red chillies, deseeded and chopped
freshly ground black pepper
3 Tbsp. olive oil

Simply combine everything in a food processor or mash together thoroughly with a fork. Do not work until completely smooth, but leave a little texture. Use at room temperature to dollop or spread. If refrigerated, the mixture will become slightly firmer. Use it up within a couple of days.

SERVES 4 OR UP TO 8 AS A GARNISH

SESAME SAUCE

Here three common ingredients are thrown together to create an uncommonly good and versatile concoction. As a sauce, it enlivens potatoes and steamed vegetables, graces any combination of salad ingredients as a dressing, and makes a scrumptious dip for the humble crudite. Serve it in a ramekin alongside *Potato and Roasted Garlic Filo Parcels* (p.44) with a selection of raw peppers, celery, cucumber, radishes and olives.

250 ml / 8 fl. oz. Greek or thick and creamy yoghurt
50g / 2 oz. sesame seeds
3 Tbsp. dark soy sauce

In a dry frying pan over moderate heat, toast the sesame seeds until they are popping and lightly browned. Transfer to a small bowl and allow to cool completely.

Stir soy sauce into the sesame seeds. Add the yoghurt and mix very thoroughly. It's best eaten on the day of preparation.

APPROXIMATELY 4 SERVINGS

SPICY RED PISTOU

Pistou is the French equivalent of pesto, and in the Provencal style, it usually consists only of basil or parsley with garlic and olive oil, and is added to soups. This version is somewhere between the French and Italian version. Whizz it up in the blender in seconds, and transform any bowl of soup into an extraordinary potage. Or, stir it into pasta or rice and heat up, drizzle over salad, mop it up with bread.

1 x 400 g / 14 oz. tin plum tomatoes, drained
3 cloves of garlic
100 g / 3 ½ oz. pine nuts, lightly toasted
a large handful of parsley, leaves stripped
1 tsp. salt
freshly ground black pepper
1 tsp. dried chilli flakes
1 Tbsp. red wine vinegar
3 Tbsp. olive oil (optional)

Blend on high speed for a few seconds. Set aside to develop flavour over a few hours.

NAPOLEON'S CHUTNEY

I'm not sure what Napoleon had to do with it, but this recipe was a standby of British housewives who were in the business of having to entertain the masses at the drop of a hat and on a shoestring. If you've never made a chutney, this will convert you to the joys of preserving: just bung it all in the pan with some vinegar and sugar, cook and bottle. Feel free to substitute ingredients with what you have to hand. I've used beetroot, carrots and squashes in place of apples, pears and apricots. Don't be alarmed by the copious amount of garlic: this is a robust and outstanding chutney.

500 g / 1 lb. cooking apples, peeled
500 g / 1 lb. pears
500 g / 1 lb. apricots (fresh or dried)
2 large green peppers
250 g / 8 oz. sultanas
2 bananas
24 cloves of garlic
2 walnut-sized pieces of root ginger
4 teaspoons garam-masala or curry powder
1 Tbsp. mild chilli powder (see *Mexican Cucumbers* p.39)
1 Tbsp. caraway seeds
2 dessertspoons salt
750 g / 1 ½ lbs. soft brown sugar
600 ml / 1 pint malt vinegar

preserving jars
heavy-bottomed stainless steel preserving pan

Preheat the oven to 160°C / 325°F / Gas 3. Cut everything up into tiny bits. (I'm afraid this has to be done by hand.)

Put everything into the pan. Bring to the boil and simmer for 40 minutes, stirring frequently with a wooden spoon.

Meanwhile, sterilise the jars. Place them on a paper towel-lined baking sheet and place in the oven for 10 minutes. If you have rubber seals, pour boiling water over them.

Spoon the hot chutney into the jars and seal. If you want to use it right away, go ahead, but it will be better after three weeks of ripening. Properly preserved , it will keep for two years before opening. After opening, store in the fridge and use within a few weeks.

YELDS ABOUT 2 KG / 4 LBS.

ROASTED RED PEPPER AND SAFFRON VINAIGRETTE

A plain plate of mixed leaves gets the royal treatment with this blinding orange vinaigrette, though it needn't be restricted to salad. The flavour is dominant, so use it sparingly, as a decorative drizzle around a plate of roasted vegetables and foliage, or with potatoes. It keeps well in the fridge for a few days.

2 red peppers
1 clove of garlic
large pinch of saffron filaments
100 ml / 3 ½ fl. oz. red wine vinegar
1 Tbsp. honey
salt and pepper to taste
100 ml / 3 ½ fl. oz. olive oil

First roast and skin your peppers. Heat the grill or oven to the highest setting. Cut the peppers in half from stem to base and remove the stem and seeds. Place cut-side-down on a baking sheet and grill or roast until blackened and blistered all over. Remove to a plastic bag, seal and leave to sweat until cool enough to handle, then peel off the papery skins.

Meanwhile, soak the saffron in a tablespoon of boiling water for at least 10 minutes to infuse.

Place everything except the oil in the blender or food processor and liquidise. Add the oil gradually to emulsify. Adjust the seasoning. It's best to leave it standing for a while to let the flavours mingle.

MAKES ABOUT 400 ML / 14 FL. OZ.

THAI SPICED BARBECUE SAUCE

Here's a thick, dark sauce with multi-dimensional flavour. Brush it on aubergine or tofu steaks, veggie burgers, vegetables skewered with mango, pineapple or Halloumi cheese, and certainly anything non-vegetarian on the barbecue. Be sure to use the correct amount of hot water to soften the coconut, or else the sauce will be too runny.

100 g / 3 ½ oz. block creamed coconut, chopped
60 ml / 2 fl. oz. boiling water
175 ml / 6 fl. oz. dark soy sauce
1 Tbsp. fish sauce
5 Tbsp. soft brown sugar
5 Tbsp. lime juice or vinegar
6 Tbsp. tomato purée
6 lime leaves, middle stem removed and finely minced
2 sticks of lemon grass, finely minced
2-3 small red chillies, snipped
2 cloves of garlic, sliced
60 ml / 2 fl. oz. sunflower or vegetable oil

Pour the boiling water over the creamed coconut and stir until smooth. Scrape into the blender jar and add everything else. Whizz on high speed until smooth, about 2 minutes. For best results, brush the sauce on your vegetables etc. at least half an hour before barbecuing so the flavours soak in. If you're using wooden skewers for kebabs, remember to soak the skewers in hot water for an hour beforehand so they don't burn on the grill.

MAKES JUST OVER 600 ML / 1 PINT

VODKA SORBET COCKTAIL

This delectable party piece has been relayed to me by an undisclosed source from Peter Sellers' butler, circa 1960. You will find it imparts a serene buzz quite unlike any other. I recommend undertaking the labour of squeezing several dozen lemons beforehand, as it's very moreish. May you revel in its lemony creaminess forever after.

I. Prepare the vodka:

Pare the rind of two lemons and drop into a bottle of fine vodka. (You will have to help yourself to a shot in order to make space.) Freeze the bottle for at least 24 hours, but preferably for a week or two—the lemon oil will turn the vodka bright yellow.

II. Prepare short cocktail glasses or champagne glasses by wetting the rims in a saucer of water and then dipping them in a saucer of white granulated sugar.

III. Fill your blender jar two-thirds full with ice. Add:

> **the juice of 8 lemons**
> **60g / 2 oz. icing sugar**
> **the desired amount of vodka. About 1/3 of a standard bottle (250 ml / 8 fl. oz.) usually does the trick**

Finally, add **one egg white** to the jar and blend at high speed for two minutes until white and frothy.

Drink immediately or reblend the remainder before serving.

MAKES ABOUT 6 SMALL COCKTAILS

SWEETS

PUMPKIN CREME CARAMEL

This hybrid has all the autumnal flavour and unique texture of pumpkin pie in a simpler format. Gigantic jack-o-lantern style pumpkins should be avoided; they are too stringy and watery. Opt for a posh pumpkin. Any family member with dense, orange, sweet flesh is suitable: butternut, acorn, kaboucha. If the pumpkin is large, I recommend roasting the whole thing, puréeing the flesh and freezing the unused portion for later use in soups, sweet and savoury tarts, and more crème caramels!

Pumpkin purée can be prepared in the following manner:

Preheat the oven to 200 °C / 400 °F / Gas 6. Cut the pumpkin in half with a large, stiff knife. Scoop out the seeds and strings with a spoon. Slice into 5 cm / 2-inch wedges from the stem to the bottom and discard the stem. Lay each wedge flesh-side-down and slice off the skin, working your way around the curve of the flesh. Place on a greased baking sheet and brush lightly with vegetable oil or melted butter. Bake for 30 to 40 minutes, until tender when prodded with a knife and lightly browned in patches. A large quantity of pumpkin may take longer to cook. Cool the pumpkin and purée in a food processor. For absolute velvetiness, you can pass the purée through a sieve.

1.5 kg / 3 lb. 4 oz. of pumpkin in its original state will yield just over 500 ml / 16 fl. oz. of purée, as required by the following recipe.

> **butter for greasing ramekins**
> **250g / 8 oz. sugar**
> **125 ml / 4 fl. oz. water**
> **500 ml / 16 fl. oz. pumpkin purée**
> **1 x 400g / 14 oz. tin sweetened condensed milk**
> **125 ml / 4 fl. oz. double cream**

125 ml / 4 fl. oz. milk
4 free-range eggs, lightly beaten
¼ tsp. salt
1 ½ tsp. pure vanilla essence
½ tsp. each of ground ginger, cinnamon and
freshly grated nutmeg

Preheat the oven to 160°C / 325°F / Gas 3. Grease 10-12 ramekins and place them in a roasting pan. Boil the kettle.

Place the sugar and water in a heavy-bottomed saucepan and stir over a low flame until the sugar dissolves. Raise the heat and let the syrup boil, without stirring, but watching it with a studying eye, until it turns a light mahogany colour. Be careful not to let it burn. Immediately divide the syrup amongst the ramekins, swirling each one to coat the bottom and sides.

Beat the rest of the ingredients together and pour into the ramekins. Pour enough hot water into the roasting pan to come half way up the sides of the ramekins. Slide carefully into the oven and bake for 30-40 minutes until set.

Remove from the *bain-marie* and leave to cool. Refrigerate for a couple of hours or overnight if desired. To serve, run a knife around just the top edge of the crème, place a plate on top of the ramekin, and flip over. Remove the ramekin, letting any spare caramel drip over the top.

FOR 10-12 INDIVIDUAL CREME CARAMELS

DYNAMITE APPLES

Make this pudding when apples are abundant and when icy cockles need warming. They're packed with sweet buttery nutmeats and fiery spices. The cayenne pepper seems to round up and activate the other spices, as well as offering its own distinctive kick. Grind your own hazelnuts if you can as pre-ground tend to taste stale. When the apples just start to explode in the oven, they're ready.

6 cooking apples
100 g / 3 ½ oz. butter
100 g / 3 ½ oz. ground hazelnuts
30 g / 1 oz. sultanas
zest of 1 lemon
3 Tbsp. soft brown sugar, plus more for sprinkling
1 tsp. ground cinnamon
¼ tsp. ground cloves
¼ tsp. cardamom seeds
¼ tsp. cayenne pepper
½ a nutmeg, grated
Greek yoghurt to serve

Preheat the oven to 220°C / 425°F / Gas 7. Grease a baking dish. Core the apples, making a 3 cm / 1 ¼ inch hole in the middle of each. A coring tool does this job neatly and quickly. Slice a bit off the bottoms of the apples so they stand up steadily, and place in the baking dish, snuggled up together.

Melt 60 g / 2 oz. of the butter and mix with the remaining ingredients. Stuff each hole with the filling, packing it in firmly. Divide the remaining butter into 6 knobs and place one on each apple. Sprinkle with a little more sugar. Bake until the flesh bursts out of the skin, about 30-40 minutes.

Remove the apples to a serving platter and scrape the buttery, nutty syrup over them. A dollop of Greek yoghurt and you're away.

SERVES 6

CHOCOLATE BANANA MASCARPONE CHEESECAKE

I think the combination of chocolate and banana is delicious. It all goes back to eating banana splits with hot fudge sauce in American ice-cream parlours as a child. The bananas for this recipe should be just ripe for eating, not o ver-ripe. This ratio of cream cheese to mascarpone always makes a better cheesecake, as plain cream cheese can be quite cloying on the palate. Try it with any cheesecake recipe. Curd cheese, which is lower in fat and in price, can be substituted for cream cheese for an even lighter result.

For the base:
200g /7 oz. plain chocolate-covered digestive biscuits
60g /2 oz. butter, melted

For the filling:
400g /14 oz. cream cheese or curd cheese
250g /9 oz. mascarpone cheese
2 large ripe bananas, sliced
2 tsp. pure vanilla essence
200g / 7 oz. caster sugar
2 free-range eggs

For the topping:
75 g /3 oz. plain chocolate
60g /2 oz butter
1 large banana, sliced slightly diagonally
juice of ½ a lemon

Preheat the oven to 180°C / 350°F / Gas 4.

Crush the chocolate biscuits in the food processor. Mix with the melted butter, then press into the bottom of a 24 cm / 9 ½ inch cake tin with a removable base. Pack it down firmly with your fingertips or smooth down with the back of a spoon. Bake the base for 10 minutes, then allow to cool. Turn the oven down to 160°C / 325°F / Gas 3.

To make the filling, whip the two cheeses together until smooth. Add the bananas, vanilla and sugar, and finally the eggs one at a time. Pour into the cake tin. Bake for 30-40 minutes until just set. If it wobbles slightly, remember that chilling will set it further.

Cool the cake in its tin on a wire rack. Then chill for at least 3 hours or overnight.

About an hour before serving, prepare the topping. Boil a small pot of water and rest a heat-proof bowl on top of it. Break up the chocolate and cut the butter into small pieces. Place them in the bowl and stir while they melt together.

Unmould the cake and place on a large serving plate. Gently smooth the chocolate mixture on top of the cake and let it ooze over the sides if you wish. Squeeze the lemon juice over the banana slices, then pat dry. This will stop them discolouring. Arrange the banana slices in the chocolate. Chill for another half hour before indulging.

8-12 SERVINGS

BLACK FOREST PAVLOVA

Pavlovas are easier than pie to make. The basic meringue, crisp on the outside and marshmallow on the inside, layered with whipped cream, is a dessert which can be manipulated into countless guises. I borrowed the German cherry-chocolate-cream combination from the famous gâteau and assigned it to the Australian classic. The result partly demonstrates Jean-Paul Sartre's interpretation of German cakes: "(They) are bulky and soft like shaving cream; they are made so that obese, easily tempted men can eat them indulgently, without worrying what they taste like but simply to fill their mouths with sweetness." In this dessert, however, the use of fresh, fat black cherries in season and quality Kirsch and chocolate, elevate it to inter-galactic gastronomic delight.

I owe the knowledge of perfect Pavlova making to Victoria Blashford-Snell and Rosie Kindersley from *Books for Cooks Cook Book No. 1*, as outlined below.

For the meringues:
6 free-range egg whites, at room temperature
a pinch of salt
360g / 12 oz. caster sugar
3 Tbsp. pure cocoa powder

For the filling and topping:
600 ml / 1 pint double cream
8 Tbsp. Kirsch liqueur
8 Tbsp. cherry compote or preserve
500g / 1 lb. fresh cherries with stems intact
60g / 2 oz. fine continental chocolate
icing sugar, mint sprigs and lavender flowers to decorate

To make the meringues, preheat the oven to 180°C / 350°F / Gas 4. Lightly grease two baking sheets and line them with parchment paper.

Choose a large whisking bowl and wash it to ensure its cleanliness, as any remnants of grease or dust will affect the process.

Dry thoroughly. Put the egg whites in it with a pinch of salt and whisk on high speed until stiff. Start sprinkling in the sugar, a tablespoon at a time, and whisk well after each spoonful. Be patient. The more gradually you add the sugar, the more likely you are to achieve a successful meringue.

Once all the sugar has been added, sift the cocoa through a small sieve and add it to the mixture, again gradually, or else you will find yourself inhaling a cloud puff of cocoa powder. Divide the mixture between the baking sheets and spread into two 20 cm / 8 inch circles. Bake for 5 minutes and then turn down the heat to 120°C / 250°F / Gas ½ and bake for 1 hour. Remove from the oven and cool completely.

Slide a long knife between the meringues and the paper and lift carefully onto a serving platter. Use the least craggy meringue as the bottom layer.

Prepare the filling. Whisk the cream until it holds its shape; do not over-whisk. Stir in the Kirsch. Spread half of the cream on the bottom meringue, top with the other meringue and the rest of the cream. Melt the chocolate in a bowl on top of a pan of simmering water or in the microwave. While hot, drizzle it over the Pavlova in fractal ribbons. Arrange the cherries on top, nestling close together with their stems standing erect. Tuck in some mint leaves and lavender blossoms and dust with icing sugar.

8-12 SERVINGS

RHUBARB FOOL AND GINGER PAVLOVA

R hubarb is abundant in spring and though short lived, it is versatile. Rhubarb fool is, in my opinion, the Original English Dessert. Rhubarb is so tart, but its delicate flavour is set off by pillows of cream and sugar. That lightness combined with a seriously sweet and textured meringue studded with ginger is a virtually royal confection.

For the fool:
1 kg / 2 lb. rhubarb, sliced into chunks
125g / 4 oz. sugar, or enough to sweeten the rhubarb
600ml / 1 pint double cream
mint sprigs and slivers of ginger to decorate

For the meringue:

Follow the recipe for *Black Forest Pavlova* (p.102), and omit the cocoa powder. Replace with 2 tsp. cornflour and 1 tsp. vinegar and add 6 pieces of stem ginger, chopped. Spread the mixture out onto a single lined baking sheet into a 30 cm / 12 inch circle. Allow room for the meringue to expand in the oven. Bake as described in the recipe.

To make the fool, stew the rhubarb and sugar together over moderate-low heat until it becomes a soft compote, about 15 minutes. Allow to cool completely. At this point you can easily push the purée through a sieve for a perfectly smooth fool if desired. Or you may prefer a slightly textured fool.

Whip the cream until it holds its shape. Fold in the rhubarb compote.

Top the baked and cooled meringue with the fool. Decorate with sprigs of mint and slivers of stem ginger.

8-12 SERVINGS

UNIVERSAL FRUIT TART

Pick a fruit, almost any fruit, and glorify it in this luscious crème fraîche custard tart. I have had particular success with red plums, nectarines, rhubarb and mango, and seedless grapes with Brazil nuts. Experiment with a hint of cardamom or nutmeg in the custard, or keep it simple. The custard does justice to any firm, ripe imagination.

500 g / 1 lb. fruit
(150 g / 5 oz. chopped nuts, optional)
1 egg white
3 egg yolks
150 g / 5 oz. crème fraîche
6 Tbsp. caster sugar or soft brown sugar
1 x 24 cm / 9 ½ inch pastry case, baked blind (see Notes p.14)

Preheat the oven to 180°C / 350°F / Gas 4. Brush the bottom of the pastry case with the egg white. This should guard against sogginess. Arrange the fruit prettily in the pastry case. (If it is a very tart fruit, sprinkle with a little extra sugar.)

Combine the crème fraîche, egg yolks and sugar and mix thoroughly. Pour over the fruit. Sprinkle on the nuts, if using.

Bake for 30-40 minutes, until golden and set. Cool for as long as possible before removing from the tin and slicing into wedges.

SERVES 8

INDEX